EYE TO EYE WITH DOGS

WEIMARANERS

Lynn M. Stone

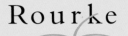

Rourke
Publishing LLC
Vero Beach, Florida 32964

www.rourkepublishing.com

PHOTO CREDITS: All photos © Lynn M. Stone

Editor: Meg Greve

Cover and page design by Nicola Stratford

Library of Congress Cataloging-in-Publication Data

Stone, Lynn M.
  Weimaraners / Lynn Stone.
    p. cm. -- (Eye to eye with dogs)
  Includes index.
  ISBN 978-1-60472-361-8
  1. Weimaraner (Dog breed)--Juvenile literature. I. Title.
  SF429.W33S76 2009
  636.752--dc22
                                        2008012974

Printed in the USA

CG/CG

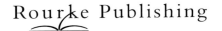

Rourke Publishing

www.rourkepublishing.com – rourke@rourkepublishing.com
Post Office Box 3328, Vero Beach, FL 32964

Table of Contents

The Weimaraner, with its smooth hair, is a favorite pet and bird hunting dog.

The Weimaraner

The Weimaraner is a large, athletic dog with wonderful hunting **instincts**. **Breeders** in Germany developed Weims for hunting. Today they are one of the most popular bird hunting **breeds** in North America. People also love them as companion dogs.

WEIMARANER FACTS

Weight: 70 to 85 pounds
(32 to 39 kilograms)
Height: 23 to 27 inches
(59 to 69 centimeters)
Country of Origin:
Germany
Life Span: 12 to 13 years

As a trained **upland** bird hunter, a Weimaraner can do it all. Its keen nose can track the scent of game bird, like a pheasant. When a running bird hides in grass, a Weim will lift a front leg to point at the bird's hiding place.

A Weimaraner tracks a pheasant to its hiding place.

With a mouth full of feathers, a Weim retrieves a pheasant.

On command, the Weim then **flushes** the bird. If the bird falls from the hunter's shot, the Weim retrieves it.

7

Looks

The Weim is a slender dog with a deep chest and short hair the color of silver. It may have a small patch of white on its chest.

The Weim's deep chest, silver hair, and floppy ears help set it apart from any other breed.

Its eyes are gray, blue, or yellowish. The sleek, silvery Weim is rarely mistaken for any other breed.

A Weimaraner has light eyes.

Whether or not a Weim has a docked tail depends upon which side of the Atlantic Ocean it lives.

A Weim has long, floppy ears, a long neck, and straight front legs. In the United States, it typically has a **docked** tail, like a boxer or Doberman pinscher. European breeders do not dock their dogs' tails.

A Weim is not a cold weather dog, but its high energy keeps it warm while dashing through the snow.

Weimaraners of the Past

Weimar, a city in Germany, inspired the name Weimaraner. Sir Duke Karl August (1757-1828) of Weimer, a breeder and hunter, originally bred the Weimaraner for hunting bear, deer, and wild boar.

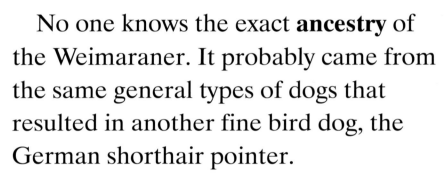

No one knows the exact **ancestry** of the Weimaraner. It probably came from the same general types of dogs that resulted in another fine bird dog, the German shorthair pointer.

One of the Weim's ancestors may have been the extinct German Leithund. Another likely ancestor is the bloodhound.

Long ago, the bloodhound may have been an ancestor of the Weimaraner.

At first, breeders called them the Weimar pointer. It was not a bird hunter. Instead, German nobles used Weims to track and chase big game animals, such as deer and wolves.

The German shorthaired pointer is a cousin of the Weimaraner.

Hunters eventually began training Weimaraners to hunt birds.

In time, big game animals became rare in Germany. Hunters then began using Weims to hunt birds.

Germany and America were at war in 1943 when the American Kennel Club accepted the Weimaraner as an established breed.

Howard Knight created American interest in the Weimaraner in the 1920s. He imported two dogs to the United States. The American Kennel Club recognized the Weimaraner as an official breed in 1943.

The Dog for You?

Weimaraners are fast, fearless, and full of energy. Once in the field, they have grace and **stamina**, and they are quick to learn. Their learning ability helps them in both field and obedience work.

Long legs and a deep chest for lung space help give the Weim speed and endurance.

If you think you want a Weimaraner, make sure you have the time. Training is important for this big, energetic dog that needs to run every day.

Training is an important part of a Weimaraner's life.

Weims love their human families.

Although Weims need a great deal of outdoor time, they love to be indoors with their human family. They are extremely loyal and affectionate.

A loyal Weimaraner has eyes only for its master.

Weims are not nearly as friendly toward strangers, either human or animal. Therefore, Weims can make fine watchdogs and guard dogs.

Do not expect a Weim to show strangers the instant love that many other sporting breeds show, such as the Labrador retriever or golden retriever.

The early Weimaraners of Germany were more aggressive dogs than they are now. American breeders have sweetened the breed's personality.

With early and careful training, this Weimaraner puppy will grow up to be an excellent hunter and loyal companion.

A Note about Dogs

Puppies are cute and cuddly, but only after serious thought should anybody buy one. Puppies, after all, grow up.

A dog will require more than love and patience. It will need healthy food, exercise, grooming, medical care, and a warm, safe place to live.

A dog can be your best friend, but you need to be its best friend, too.

Choosing the right breed for you requires homework. For more information about buying and owning a dog, contact the American Kennel Club or the Canadian Kennel Club.

Glossary

ancestry (AN-sess-tree): the animals that at some past time were part of the modern animal's family

breeds (BREEDS): particular kinds of domestic animals within a larger, closely related groups, such as the Weimaraner within the dog group

breeders (BREED-urz): those who keep adult dogs and raise their pups, especially those who do so regularly and with great care

docked (DOKT): to have a section (or all) of the tail removed

flushes (FLUHSH-iz): chases from hiding; chases into flight

instincts (IN-stingkts): abilities or desires animals and people are born with, not taught

stamina (STAM-uh-nuh): the ability to keep going

upland (UHP-land): on land, especially in reference to game birds of fields and forests

Index

Further Reading

Averis, Gillian. *Weimaraner*. Ringpress, 2002.
Cuneo, Anitra and Roy. *Weimaraner*. Kennel Clubs Books, 2004.
Zwaschka, Michael. *The Weimaraner*. Coughlan, 1999.

Website to Visit

www.akc.org/breeds/weimaraner/index.cfm
www.weimclubamerica.org
www.canismajor.com/dog/weimar.html

About the Author

Lynn M. Stone is a widely-published wildlife and domestic animal
photographer and the author of more than 500 children's books.
His book *Box Turtles* was chosen as an Outstanding Science Trade
Book and Selectors' Choice for 2008 by the Science Committee of
the National Science Teachers' Association and the Children's
Book Council.